Sunny
Thoughts

Blue Mountain Arts®

Bestselling Titles

By Susan Polis Schutz:
To My Daughter, with Love, on the Important Things in Life
To My Son with Love

By Douglas Pagels:
42 Gifts I'd Like to Give to You
100 Things to Always Remember… and One Thing to Never Forget
May You Always Have an Angel by Your Side
To the One Person I Consider to Be My Soul Mate

Is It Time to Make a Change?
by Deanna Beisser

To the Love of My Life
by Donna Fargo

Anthologies:
Always Believe in Yourself and Your Dreams
For You, My Daughter
Friends for Life
Hang In There
I Love You, Mom
I'm Glad You Are My Sister
The Joys and Challenges of Motherhood
The Language of Recovery
Marriage Is a Promise of Love
Teaching and Learning Are Lifelong Journeys
There Is Greatness Within You, My Son
Think Positive Thoughts Every Day
Thoughts to Share with a Wonderful Teenager
True Wealth
With God by Your Side …You Never Have to Be Alone
You're Just like a Sister to Me

Sunny Thoughts

Words to Keep You Smiling, Shining, and Looking on the Bright Side

Written and Edited by
Suzanne Moore

Blue Mountain Press™
Boulder, Colorado

Library of Congress Control Number: 2005900764
ISBN: 0-88396-925-4

Certain trademarks are used under license.
BLUE MOUNTAIN PRESS is registered in U.S. Patent and Trademark Office.

Printed in the United States of America.
First Printing: 2005

 This book is printed on recycled paper.

This book is printed on fine quality, laid embossed, 80 lb. paper. This paper has been specially produced to be acid free (neutral pH) and contains no groundwood or unbleached pulp. It conforms with the requirements of the American National Standards Institute, Inc., so as to ensure that this book will last and be enjoyed by future generations.

Blue Mountain Arts, Inc.

P.O. Box 4549, Boulder, Colorado 80306

Contents

(Authors listed in order of first appearance)

Introduction

Everyone has those days when it feels like the sun has forgotten to shine — days when nothing feels right and the world seems to be filled with more stress and difficulties than happiness. The good news is that no matter what happens, you can choose to make it better. Whether you're facing one of life's big obstacles or just having a bad day, there are so many little things you can do to cheer yourself up.

Think of this book as a dose of inspiration, filled with thoughts and ideas to keep you smiling, shining, and looking on the bright side. Next time you need a little pick-me-up, flip it open to any page and read whatever catches your eye. Whether you need a funny quote to make you smile, a piece of practical advice for getting rid of the blues, or an inspiring message to remind you that you're strong enough to weather any storm, you'll find it here. Let each word be like a little ray of sunshine waiting to sweep away those clouds and brighten your day.

A cloudy day is no match
for a sunny disposition.

— William Arthur Ward

Don't Let Life
Rain on Your Parade

Every day, from the moment you wake up until the
moment you fall asleep, you have a choice: you can let
your mood dictate your day or you can let your day
dictate your mood. Your attitude affects the way you see
the world, and if you decide to be in a good mood no
matter what, you'll find that life looks a whole lot brighter.

When you get out of bed, decide that you're going to have
a great day. Choose to be happy and don't let life's little
problems get you down. If you're driving down the street
and someone cuts you off, just slow down and let them
through. Turn up the radio and be glad you're not in as
much of a hurry as they are. If you get to work and find
there's no milk left for your coffee, don't take it as a sign
that the day is doomed. Just drink tea instead. Pay attention
to how nice it can be to have something a little different
from your usual.

It's easy to get into a bad mood if you let life decide what
kind of day you'll have, because life will never be perfect.
So just accept the fact that some rain clouds will come your
way every once in a while, and do your best not to let a
few little drops dampen your spirit.

Choose Happiness

I am more and more convinced that our happiness or our unhappiness depends far more on the way we meet the events of life than on the nature of those events themselves.

— Karl Wilhelm von Humboldt

Most folks are just about as happy as they make up their minds to be.

— Abraham Lincoln

The happiness habit is developed by simply practicing happy thinking. Make a mental list of happy thoughts and pass them through your mind several times every day.... Savor their joy. Such thoughts will help cause events to turn out that way.

— Norman Vincent Peale

The way you live your life, the perspective you select, is a choice you make every single day when you wake up. It's yours to decide.

— Lance Armstrong

We've all had bad days when stuff kept happening and wondered, "Oh no, what next?" Don't let it throw you off track. Just keep repeating the mantra... It's not what happens to me that's important — it's how I respond to what happens.

— John Alston and Lloyd Thaxton

The next time life gets you down, remember, you have a choice. You can either stay down in the doldrums where there is nothing but more negative feelings, or you can make up your mind to laugh until the doldrums disappear. The choice is up to you. Find a reason to laugh!

— Les Brown

*Like a welcome summer rain,
humor may suddenly
cleanse and cool the earth,
the air, and you.*

— Langston Hughes

Lighten Up!

Have you ever noticed that the funniest movies are the ones where everything goes wrong? From the classic comedies of Buster Keaton and Charlie Chaplin to modern-day comedians like Jim Carrey and Jerry Seinfeld, it's easy to see that the funniest things in life are the problems, irritations, and annoyances we face.

Next time you find yourself having one of those horrible, no good, very bad days, remind yourself not to take life so seriously. Laugh at yourself when you make a mistake. Laugh at life when it throws you every curveball imaginable. Laugh when you can't find your keys, when you fall down and get a hole in your new pants, or when you miss winning the lottery by one little number. Ever heard the saying "You'll look back at this and laugh one day"? Why bother waiting? Go ahead and laugh about it now!

Just for Laughs...

Into each life some rain must fall.
Usually the day after you wash your car.

They say money can't make you happy.
All I ask is a chance to prove them wrong.

If I won the lottery, I wouldn't quit my job
right away. I'd rub it in my co-workers' faces
for a couple weeks first.

Nobody's perfect. If they were, there
wouldn't be anyone to make fun of.

Always forgive your enemies.
Nothing could irritate them more.

Every rose has its thorn. So if you're going
to steal flowers from the neighbor's garden,
make sure to put on thick gloves first.

Without the rain, there would be no rainbow.
But since that pot of gold thing is just a myth,
who really needs a rainbow anyway?

It takes fewer muscles to smile than to frown,
and even fewer to ignore someone completely.

Don't walk behind me, for I may not lead.
Don't walk ahead of me, for I may not follow.
Don't walk beside me, either. Just go away.

Five Reasons
to Cheer Up

1. People will stop saying annoying things like
   "Smile" and "It can't be *that* bad."

2. Attitudes are contagious, and the better mood
   you're in, the better mood people around you
   will be in.

3. Smile lines are much more attractive than
   frown lines.

4. For every bad thing that happens, you learn
   something new and grow as a person. So the
   worse things are today, the closer to being a
   genius you'll be tomorrow.

5. Even the darkest day is only twenty-four hours.

— Carol Thomas

Some Days Are Better than Others

Some days are all dreaming in the sun.
Some days are chocolate sundaes,
returned phone calls, right answers.
Some days you just walk down the street and
everything seems to be going your way...

Other days — when you sit on the gum wad
stuck to the seat of your economy car,
late for work, or late for something else
that must be important —
drivers honking at you,
drivers yelling at you —
on those days,
remember the other, sunshiney days,
and pray for their swift return.

— Ashley Rice

"Rainy-Day" Remedies

When life gets overwhelming, remember that there are always things you can do to make it better. Sometimes the simplest things are the ones that work the best. Lace up your sneakers and go for a run. Snuggle up under a blanket and watch a great movie. Talk for hours to a good friend. And of course, you must never forget the most powerful remedy of all: lots and lots of chocolate.

— Rachyl Taylor

My advice is: "Go outside, to the country, enjoy the sun and all nature has to offer. Go outside and try to recapture the happiness within yourself; think of all the beauty in yourself and in everything around you and be happy."

— Anne Frank

Anytime you're feeling a little down, remember that things could always be worse. If by some unfortunate chance they *do* get worse, you can take comfort in the knowledge that things are so bad they have to get better.

— Carol Thomas

If I were asked to give what I consider the single most useful bit of advice for all humanity it would be this: Expect trouble as an inevitable part of life and, when it comes, hold your head high, look it squarely in the eye and say, "I will be bigger than you. You cannot defeat me." Then repeat to yourself the most comforting of all words, "This too shall pass."

— Ann Landers

A good exercise is to try to approach a single day without expectations. Don't expect people to be friendly. When they're not, you won't be surprised or bothered. If they are, you'll be delighted. Don't expect your day to be problem free. Instead, as problems come up, say to yourself, "Ah, another hurdle to overcome." As you approach your day in this manner you'll notice how graceful life can be. Rather than fighting against life, you'll be dancing with it. Pretty soon, with practice, you'll lighten up your entire life. And when you lighten up, life is a lot more fun.

— Richard Carlson, PhD

Resolve to see the world on the sunny side, and you have almost won the battle of life at the outset.

— Sir Roger L'Estrange

Look on the Bright Side

There's an old saying that tells us we can either be upset that roses have thorns, or grateful that thorns have roses. This simple little philosophy may sound a bit cliché, but it also makes one thing clear: while your thinking may not actually change anything in the grand scheme of life... it can change *everything* in the grand scheme of *your* life.

When things aren't going the way you'd like, remind yourself that every negative has a positive somewhere in it. If you didn't get the job offer you were hoping for, maybe there's an even better one waiting down the road. If you've been in bed with the flu for a week, maybe you'll realize what a gift your health is.

The way you look at things can make your whole world seem different, even if nothing has changed but your perspective. So go ahead, take off those dark shades and put on some rose-colored ones. You'll be amazed at how much brighter the world appears.

Thoughts from the Bright Side

My barn having burned to the ground,
I can now see the moon.

— Taoist Saying

I'm not afraid of storms, for
I'm learning to sail my ship.

— Louisa May Alcott

Clouds come floating into my life, no
longer to carry rain or usher storm, but
to add color to my sunset sky.

— Rabindranath Tagore

Keep your face
to the sunshine
and you cannot
see the shadow.

— Helen Keller

Pain is inevitable;
suffering is optional.

— Author Unknown

I don't think about all the misery, but
about the beauty that still remains.

— Anne Frank

Optimism: Taking Life Sunny-Side Up

Optimism isn't pretending life is perfect
It's rising above whatever comes your way
It's finding the silver lining in those
  big, dark clouds
And knowing there's a rainbow for every
  rainy day

It's more than thinking the glass is half full
It's being thankful there's a glass there at all
It's taking life's problems with a smile and
  some strength
It's being brave, being happy, standing tall

So next time your day seems dark and dreary
Remember there's so much you can do
You can brighten your skies and lighten
  your heart
The choice is up to you

— Natalie Evans

Real optimism is aware of problems
but recognizes the solutions, knows
about difficulties but believes they can
be overcome, sees the negatives but
accentuates the positives, is exposed to
the worst but expects the best, has reason
to complain but chooses to smile.

— William Arthur Ward

I have become my own version of an optimist.
If I can't make it through one door, I'll go through
another door — or I'll make a door. Something
terrific will come no matter how dark the present.

— Rabindranath Tagore

A pessimist sees only the dark side
of the clouds and mopes; a philosopher
sees both sides and shrugs; an optimist
doesn't see the clouds at all — he's
walking on them.

— D. O. Flynn

The Optimist's Creed

Promise Yourself:

To be so strong that nothing can disturb your peace of mind.

To talk health, happiness, and prosperity to every person you meet.

To make all your friends feel that there is something in them.

To look at the sunny side of everything and make your optimism come true.

To think only of the best, to work only for the best, and to expect only the best.

To be just as enthusiastic about the success of others as you are about your own.

To forget the mistakes of the past and press on to the greater achievements of the future.

To wear a cheerful countenance at all times and give every living creature you meet a smile.

To give so much time to the improvement of yourself that you have no time to criticize others.

To be too large for worry, too noble for anger, too strong for fear, and too happy to permit the presence of trouble.

— Christian D. Larson

Just by changing your attitude,
you have the power to turn
rainy days into rainbows.

— Natalie Evans

I watch people who let a headache ruin their
day. Things like a flat tire, busy phone lines,
and crying babies give some people ulcers.
Marital spats, financial troubles, and canceled
flights give people high blood pressure. But I
have to tell you. To me those things are no
big deal. I'm just happy to be here!

— John F. Northcott

Anywhere is paradise;
it's up to you.

— Author Unknown

Life is beautiful music;
some high notes,
some low notes,
but beautiful just the same.

— Author Unknown

It's a Beautiful Life

Happiness is more than a mood or a feeling; it's a way of life, one that doesn't change with the weather. True happiness might be dimmed when rainy days come along, but it never disappears. If you hold on to those wonderful qualities that are filled with so much light — like hope, faith, and an optimistic outlook — you can see yourself through anything life brings.

You can be happy, rain or shine, once you understand that the only place you'll ever find happiness... is right inside you. Happiness begins at the point of acceptance: the point when you stop questioning why life can't be perfect and just accept the world the way it is. It's the point when you stop looking for a neatly wrapped happily-ever-after or a magical Garden of Eden. The real world is full of joys, and some pains, too, but when you realize that it all balances out, you become free to enjoy life for what it is. And what it is... is a beautiful symphony of highs and lows, rainbows that follow the rain, and a sun that will always be there, ready to shine again.

How to Find Happiness...

Happiness is a way of life — an overriding outlook composed of qualities such as optimism, courage, love, and fulfillment. It's not just tiptoeing through the tulips of la-la land, and it's not something that changes every time your situation changes. It is nothing less than cherishing every day.

— Dan Barker, PhD

Happiness cannot come from without. It must come from within. It is not what we see and touch or that which others do for us which makes us happy; it is that which we think and feel and do, first for the other fellow and then for ourselves.

— Helen Keller

Happiness is not something you can find like a stone in the road that has a beautiful color. It is the by-product of your being completely yourself and being very much aware, and it can happen at any moment.

— May Sarton

They say happiness is a thing you can't see,
A thing you can't touch — I disagree.
Happiness is standing beside me.
Happiness is whatever you want it to be.
Happiness is a high hill;
Will I find it — yes I will.
Happiness is a tall tree,
Can I climb it — watch and see.
Happiness is whatever you want it to be.

— Leslie Bricusse

*Our brightest blazes
are commonly kindled
by unexpected sparks.*

— Samuel Johnson

Little Rays of Sunshine

When we think about what would make us happy, we generally think of big things: buying our dream home, getting a huge raise, having children, or finally taking that perfect vacation. What we need to remember is that while the big things only come along once in a while, there are thousands of little things that have the power to bring that same sense of joy to our hearts — if we will only take the time to stop and enjoy them. From finding a great parking spot to enjoying a short walk on a beautiful summer day, there are tiny bits of happiness all around you, just waiting for you to scoop them up.

Instead of always living in anticipation of the big things, take time to notice the little things that make you happy every day. Then do whatever you can to put more of them into your life. You'll find that even the cloudiest of days has a few rays of sunshine hidden inside... if you're willing to open your heart and look.

"The Little Roads to Happiness"

The little roads to happiness,
    they are not hard to find;
They do not lead to great success —
    but to a quiet mind.
They do not lead to mighty power,
    nor to substantial wealth.
They bring one to a book, a flower,
    a song of cheer and health.
The little roads to happiness are free
    to everyone;
They lead one to the wind's caress,
    to kiss of friendly sun.
These little roads are shining white,
    for all the world to see;
Their sign-boards, pointing left and right,
    are love and sympathy.
The little roads of happiness have this
    most charming way;
No matter how they may digress
    throughout the busy day;
No matter where they twist and wind
    through fields of rich delight,
They're always of the self same mind
    to lead us home at night.

— Wilhelmina Stitch

It's the little things which
keep the world shining —
little beams by day and
little twinkles by night.

— Leroy Brownlow

Sometimes it's the little things that mean the
most: the song of a bird, a warm breeze blowing
through the trees, a friendly voice on the other
end of a telephone, a note written by a friend to
us when we need encouragement, the wag of a
dog's tail as we come home from a hard day at
work. These things are intangible — we cannot
put a price tag on what they mean to us or how
they help us to feel abiding peace even in the
midst of turmoil.

— Heather Parkins

Quick Pick-Me-Ups
for When Life Gets You Down

1. Get outside and let nature heal you. If it's a sunny day, have a picnic in the park. If it's snowing, bundle up and make a snowman or a snow angel. No matter what the weather, being outside in the natural world is a great way to reconnect with what really matters.

2. Fake it. If you force yourself to pretend you're in a great mood, before you know it, it'll become reality.

3. Get creative. Remember when rainy days used to mean it was time for arts and crafts? Try immersing yourself in something creative, like pottery, drawing, knitting, or writing It will help get your mind off whatever's bothering you and give you a sense of purpose and achievement.

4. Treat yourself. Whether it's something as simple as an ice-cream cone or as indulgent as a massage, treat yourself to something that will make you feel good.

5. Go for a drive. There's something about the open road that tempts us to leave all our problems behind and drive off into the sunset. So why not give it a try? The only rule is that you must have no destination in mind; simply follow the road wherever it leads you. Roll down the windows, turn up the radio, and drive until the world makes sense again.

6. Clean! Taking out your frustration on the grungy tub is a great way to relieve stress, and when you're done, you can hop in for a relaxing bath.

7. Have a good cry. Some of us spend a lot of energy trying to hold in the things that are bothering us, but some days you need to just let go of it all. Give yourself permission to feel sorry for yourself and break down in tears. When you've cried until there are no tears left, you'll feel drained but refreshed. You'll feel ready to face the world and begin again.

8. Get in the kitchen and cook something delicious. Whether you prepare a five-course meal or some classic comfort food, you'll find that gathering the ingredients, chopping, and stirring have an amazingly soothing effect. And that's not to mention the pleasure you'll get from eating your creation when it's done!

9. Dance. It doesn't matter if you go to a popular nightclub or just let loose in the middle of your living room. Once you get your body moving, you'll find it's impossible to stay in a bad mood.

10. Vent. Your friends and family are there to listen when things go wrong, to pick you up when you're feeling down, and to remind you how great you are and that you deserve nothing but the best. Take advantage of the opportunity for free counseling and pour your heart out to a loved one the next time it's feeling a bit heavy. Whether or not they have the answers to your problems, you're sure to feel better just getting it all off your chest.

Singing in the Rain

Music is a prescription that can cure almost any bad mood. It has a way of taking your mind off whatever is bothering you, speaking directly to your spirit, and lifting you up almost instantly. Next time you find yourself feeling a little blue, try putting on some upbeat music. Before you know it, you'll find yourself singing along, and chances are, you'll have forgotten all about whatever was bringing you down.

If you need a little added inspiration, check out the optimistic messages in any of these cheer-inducing songs...

"I Feel Good"
by James Brown

"Walking on Sunshine"
by Katrina and the Waves

"I Can See Clearly Now"
by Johnny Nash

"Here Comes the Sun"
by The Beatles

"Don't Worry, Be Happy"
by Bobby McFerrin

"Beautiful Day"
by U2

Movie Magic

If you're having one of those days when you want to escape from the real world, give yourself permission to do just that. Put your feet up, grab a cozy blanket, and let the Hollywood stars get to work lifting your spirits. Whether you go for a comedy that will make you laugh out loud or a classic with an inspiring message, you're sure to find yourself feeling better soon.

Try one of these suggestions, or rent your own personal favorite...

The Sound of Music

It's a Wonderful Life

Happy Gilmore

Big

Spaceballs

The Wizard of Oz

Caddyshack

The Money Pit

Shrek I and *II*

The Princess Bride

Monty Python and the Holy Grail

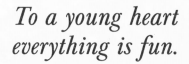

To a young heart
everything is fun.

— Charles Dickens

Splash in the Puddles

Studies have shown that children laugh an average of four hundred times per day, while adults measure in at just fifteen. That's a pretty depressing statistic that can't help but make you wonder... What do kids know that we don't?

The answer is, they know how to have fun. They know how to go swimming without worrying about how they look in their bathing suits, how to find wonder and magic in something as simple as a ladybug, and how to entertain themselves for hours with no company other than an imaginary friend.

Most of us know how to do these things, too, but we've forgotten somewhere along the road to adulthood. Life will always have responsibilities and things that need to get done, but we should all remind ourselves that the most important thing about life isn't checking every item off our to-do lists. It's enjoying ourselves along the way.

Remind yourself how important it is to have fun, and then go have some. Turn the page for a few ideas to get you in the mood...

Ten Ways to Have Some Fun!

Go to the park, swing on the swings, and slide down the slide.

Lie down on the grass on a sunny day and look for shapes in the clouds.

Find a dandelion and make a wish.

Run for the sheer joy of running, not to lose weight or to get in shape or to catch a bus.

Jump in a big, wet, muddy puddle after the next big storm.

Go home and make a huge mess, and don't even think about cleaning it up until tomorrow.

Jump on the bed.

Watch cartoons on Saturday morning.

Pull all the cushions off the couch and build a fort.

Go somewhere kids are and watch them play. Let them inspire you!

It's never too late to have
a happy childhood.

— Author Unknown

He who does not get fun and
enjoyment out of every day...
needs to reorganize his life.

— George Matthew Adams

If we are ever to enjoy life, now is the
time. Today should always be our most
wonderful day.

— Thomas Dreier

The world always
looks brighter
from behind a smile.

— Author Unknown

Put on a Happy Face

Some days the smiles might come a little easier, and other days you might have to look a little harder to find them, but the key is to keep looking for them, even when they seem far away.

If you're having a tough day at work, take a break to get a paper and look through the funnies. If things at home seem chaotic, escape to the bathroom and immerse yourself in bubbles and hot water. You can always give yourself something to smile about — no matter how small it may be.

Think of things that make you smile and make sure you put at least one on your to-do list every day. Whether you take a trip to the pet store, put on your favorite sweater, or treat yourself to a little mid-afternoon chocolate, make sure you find time for at least one smile a day. It's good for your health, good for your looks, and good for your heart. So go ahead and find something to smile about!

A Smile a Day
Keeps the Clouds Away

You can smile
because you're happy...
or you can be happy
because you smile.

— Tyler Richards

Start off every day with a smile
and get it over with.

— W. C. Fields

Life is never so bad you can't find something
to smile about.

— George Foreman

What sunshine is to flowers,
smiles are to humanity.

— Joseph Addison

For no reason at all except that it will make
you a happier person, smile. Smile at a perfect
stranger, at your beloved, at a child whose
parents are too busy or too preoccupied to
smile. Show your teeth — especially if you
haven't got any. Smile when you see someone
or something you like. Smile broadly, demurely,
shyly, mysteriously. Smile from ear to ear. Smile
at the bus driver, smile at the toll taker, smile at
the stressed-out driver at the stoplight. Make
them all wonder, "What's she smiling about?"
Let them wonder. Let a smile be your umbrella
on a rainy day.

— Rachel Snyder

Cheerfulness is contagious,
but don't wait to catch it from
someone else. Be a carrier!

— Author Unknown

Spread Some Sunshine

Happiness defies the laws of arithmetic: the more you give away, the more you get in return. Doing something for someone else is a sure-fire way to give your spirit a lift. Just remember that the things you do don't have to be grand, sweeping gestures. The little things can make just as much of a difference.

When you go to a store, be a little nicer to the clerks who help you. Smile and look them in the eye, and be the first one to say "Have a nice day." When you go to work, make a conscious effort to be more positive. Praise your co-workers, say "thank you" often, and be friendly and outgoing. It will make their day better, but you'll quickly see that it makes your day much nicer, too!

Spreading some sunshine into the lives of others can't help but brighten your days as well. You'll feel good about yourself, good about others, and good about life. And what could be better than that?

Ten Simple Ways
to Brighten Someone's Day

Buy some chocolates and leave one on everyone's desk at work.

Smile at a stranger on the street.

Give someone a compliment.

Add happy faces to all the e-mails you send out.

Lend a friend one of your favorite books or videos.

Let somebody with fewer items go ahead of you in line at the store.

Clean the house, even if it's not your turn.

Send a greeting card for no reason.

Pay the toll for the car behind you.

Tell someone how much you love them.

Happiness is like jelly; you can't
spread even a little bit without getting
some on yourself.

— Author Unknown

A single sunbeam is enough
to drive away many shadows.

— Saint Francis of Assisi

A smile, a sharing of the joys of the sunrise
and sunset, perhaps teaching a small child to
ride a bike or fly a kite... these are what counts
in a lifetime.

— Ruth Fishel

There is always something
for which to be thankful.

— Charles Dickens

The Gratitude Attitude

One of the biggest keys to happiness is learning to appreciate what you have. So many of us dream of better lives — more money, bigger houses, better relationships — and we think that once we attain those ideals, we will be happy.

It's okay to have dreams, but it's not okay to keep postponing happiness while you're waiting for them to come true. Unfortunately, whatever it is that you think will make you happy probably won't. Once you buy that house you've been dreaming of, you're sure to start imagining how happy you'll be once you pay off your mortgage. Lose those ten pounds and you'll probably start thinking you'd look even better if you lost just a little more.

Real happiness doesn't come from having all your dreams come true. It comes from realizing you already have everything you need. Next time you're feeling a little down, try making a list of some of the things you're grateful for. Focus on those blessings instead of the few things that aren't going your way. The more grateful you are for the blessings you have in your life, the more good things you'll find. So open your eyes, open your heart, and look for a little sunshine today. It's all around you.

Your Pot of Gold

Contentment is not the fulfillment of
what you want, but the realization
of how much you already have.

— Author Unknown

We all possess things which we would never sell for
even the worth of the highest lottery, so why don't
we celebrate? I'm referring to the wonderful gifts we
receive every day. We wake up, we can see, we have
mobility, we can breathe... and literally thousands of
functions which we take completely for granted
without a thought. Aren't these functions more vital
to us than any sum of wealth? We know they are,
because we have all seen what it's like when some of
these functions don't work correctly. Yet we still
often find reason to be disillusioned despite the fact
that we win the lottery in the biggest way each time
we awake, and each time we draw a breath.

— Rabbi Chaim Dovid Green

Appreciating life doesn't mean having
to believe that everything happens for the
best. I tell people to look for the good in
life, not the best. The best doesn't always
happen. But good, in one form or another,
always does. And good is good enough.

— Dan Baker, PhD

The truth is, we see in life what we want to see.
If you search for ugliness you'll find plenty of it.
If you want to find fault with other people, your
career, or the world in general, you'll certainly be
able to do so. But the opposite is also true. If you
look for the extraordinary in the ordinary, you can
train yourself to see it.

— Richard Carlson, PhD

Look for something to be thankful and
glad over each day, and you will find it.

— Ella Wheeler Wilcox

*Today is the tomorrow
you were optimistic about
yesterday.*

— Zig Ziglar

Rise and Shine

There is nothing more optimistic than the thought of a new day — a brand-new beginning filled with the promise of hope and unlimited potential.

Unfortunately, when the day actually dawns, most of us don't think of it quite that optimistically. Too many of us often think of tomorrow as the day filled with hope, while today becomes loaded down with chores, responsibilities, and unfulfilled promises. Starting today, you have a chance to change all that. You can make today everything you've always dreamed your tomorrows would be.

When the alarm clock goes off, resist the urge to push the snooze button. Get out of bed, be grateful for a fresh start, and wonder what exciting things the new day will bring. Rise and shine... and keep on shining. Whatever you promised yourself you'd do yesterday, get to it. Appreciate the day for all that it is, all that it isn't, and all that it can be. Be grateful for every minute, even those early-morning, un-sunshiney ones. Make today the day you were so hopeful about yesterday. If not today, then when?

"Today I Smiled"

Today I smiled, and all at once
Things didn't look so bad.
Today I shared with someone else
A little bit of hope I had.

Today I sang a little song,
And felt my heart grow light.
I walked a happy little mile
With not a cloud in sight.

Today I worked with what I had
And longed for nothing more,
And what had seemed like only weeds
Were flowers at my door.

Today I loved a little more
And complained a little less.
And in the giving of myself,
I forgot my weariness.

— Author Unknown

Write it on your heart that every day
is the best day of the year.

> — Ralph Waldo Emerson

To live another day again comes down
to living and enjoying the process.
The excitement of life really lies in living
to such an extent that it's wonderful to
breathe a little fresh air, to see the rain,
to have a good meal, to dunk a doughnut
in some skimmed milk, and to live with
everything that there is.

> — Theodore Isaac Rubin, MD

I have come to the conclusion
that you have to live every day,
do your best every day,
enjoy every day.
Each day is a little life.

> — Alfred A. Montapert

Keep Shining!

Everybody has slumps. Hitters and pitchers struggle for no reason. Your good moods suddenly become bad moods. Who knows why?... All you can do is keep the faith and keep working hard and hope that your luck changes.

— Yogi Berra

The reality of life is that you deal with your circumstances as they come to you. You do the best you can, you try to stay in a positive mindset, and... you hang in there because "Tomorrow's another day."

— Erin Brockovich

You have the power
to do something even
the great sun cannot do:
you can shine in the
darkest of night.

— Author Unknown

Everyone in life goes through a hard time sometime, but you can't let that define who you are. What defines you is how you come back from those troubles and what you find in life to smile about.

— George Foreman

The way to happiness: keep your heart free from hate, your mind from worry. Live simply, expect little, give much. Fill your life with love. Scatter sunshine. Forget self, think of others. Do as you would be done by. Try this for a week and you will be surprised.

— Norman Vincent Peale

So onward and upward, with renewed spirits!

— Anne Frank

If the sun forgets
to shine on your day,
don't let it get you down.
Just smile and
brighten it yourself.

— Charlotte Morrison

Be the Sun
in Your Own Sky

Life will always have its share of rainy days, but the great part is that you get to decide what to do with them. You can let dark clouds and problems get you down... or you can decide to be the sun in your own sky. If you keep on shining no matter what comes your way, it won't be long before a rainbow appears.

No matter how dark your day seems, just remember that you can make it brighter. Look beyond the clouds and know that the sun is still shining behind them. Think sunny thoughts. Chase away your tears with a smile. Find an umbrella and remind yourself that a rainbow is in the making. Whatever life brings your way, in the end, the choice is always yours. You can be anything you want to be. And that includes happy.

ACKNOWLEDGMENTS

We gratefully acknowledge the permission granted by the following authors, publishers, and authors' representatives to reprint poems or excerpts from their publications.

Simon & Schuster Adult Publishing Group for "The happiness habit..." and "The way to happiness..." from THE POWER OF POSITIVE THINKING by Norman Vincent Peale. Copyright © 1952, 1956 by Prentice-Hall, Inc., copyrights renewed 1980, 1984 by Norman Vincent Peale. All rights reserved. And for "If I were asked to give..." from SINCE YOU ASK ME by Ann Landers. Copyright © 1961 by Ann Landers. All rights reserved. And for "Life is never so bad..." and "Everyone in life goes..." from GEORGE FOREMAN'S GUIDE TO LIFE by George Foreman. Copyright © 2002 by George Foreman. All rights reserved. And for "I have come to the..." from INSPIRATION & MOTIVATION by Alfred A. Montapert. Copyright © 1982 by Alfred Armand Montapert. All rights reserved.

Broadway Books, a division of Random House, Inc., for "The way you live your life..." from EVERY SECOND COUNTS by Lance Armstrong. Copyright © 2003 by Lance Armstrong. All rights reserved.

John Wiley & Sons, Inc., for "We've all had bad days..." from STUFF HAPPENS by John Alston and Lloyd Thaxton. Copyright © 2003 by John Alston and Lloyd Thaxton. All rights reserved.

Les Brown Enterprises for "The next time life gets..." from UP THOUGHTS FOR DOWN TIMES by Les Brown. Copyright © 2003 by Les Brown Enterprises. All rights reserved.

Harold Ober Associates Incorporated for "Like a welcome summer rain..." from "A Note on Humor" from THE BOOK OF NEGRO HUMOR by Langston Hughes. Copyright © 1966 by Langston Hughes. All rights reserved.

Doubleday, a division of Random House, Inc., for "My advice is...," "I don't think about all the misery...," and "So onward and upward..." from THE DIARY OF A YOUNG GIRL: THE DEFINITIVE EDITION by Anne Frank. Otto H. Frank & Mirjam Presser, Editors, translated by Susan Massotty, copyright © 1995 by Doubleday, a division of Random House, Inc. All rights reserved.

Hyperion for "A good exercise is to try to..." and "The truth is, we see in life..." from DON'T SWEAT THE SMALL STUFF... AND IT'S ALL SMALL STUFF by Richard Carlson, PhD. Copyright © 1997 by Richard Carlson, PhD. Reprinted by permission. All rights reserved. And for "Everybody has..." from WHEN YOU COME TO A FORK IN THE ROAD, TAKE IT! by Yogi Berra with Dave Kaplan. Copyright © 2001 by Yogi Berra. Reprinted by permission. All rights reserved.

Penguin Group (USA), Inc., for "I watch people who let..." by John F. Northcott from TAKE IT FROM ME, edited by Michael Levine. Copyright © 1996 by Michael Levine. All rights reserved.

Rodale, Inc., Emmaus, PA 18908, www.rodalestore.com, for "Happiness is a way of life..." and "Appreciating life..." from WHAT HAPPY PEOPLE KNOW: HOW THE NEW SCIENCE OF HAPPINESS CAN CHANGE YOUR LIFE FOR THE BETTER by Dan Baker, PhD. Copyright © 2003 by Dan Baker, PhD, and Cameron Stauth. All rights reserved.

Dennis Wholey for "Happiness is not something...." by May Sarton and "To live another day again..." by Theodore Isaac Rubin, MD, from ARE YOU HAPPY?, edited by Dennis Wholey. Copyright © 1986 by Dennis Wholey. All rights reserved.

Cherry River Music, Inc., for "They say happiness is a thing..." from "Happiness" from SCROOGE by Leslie Bricusse. Copyright © 1992 by Leslie Bricusse. All rights reserved.

The Brownlow Corporation for "It's the little things..." from TODAY IS MINE by Leroy Brownlow. Copyright © 1972 by Leroy Brownlow. All rights reserved.

Heather Parkins for "Sometimes it's the little things that mean..." from "Peace Begins Within." Copyright © 2000 by Heather Parkins. All rights reserved.

McGraw-Hill, a division of The McGraw-Hill Companies, for "For no reason at all..." from 365 WORDS OF WELL-BEING FOR WOMEN by Rachel Snyder. Copyright © 1997 by Rachel Snyder. All rights reserved. And for "The reality of life is that..." from TAKE IT FROM ME by Erin Brockovich. Copyright © 2002 by Erin Brockovich. All rights reserved.

Health Communications, Inc., for "A smile, a sharing..." from TIME FOR JOY by Ruth Fishel. Copyright © 1988 by Ruth Fishel. All rights reserved.

Rabbi Chaim Dovid Green for "We all possess things..." from torah.org. Copyright © 1998 by Rabbi Chaim Dovid Green. All rights reserved.

Thomas Nelson, Inc., Nashville, TN, for "Today is the tomorrow..." from SOMETHING ELSE TO SMILE ABOUT by Zig Ziglar. Copyright © 1999 by the Zig Ziglar Corporation. All rights reserved.

A careful effort has been made to trace the ownership of selections used in this anthology in order to obtain permission to reprint copyrighted material and give proper credit to the copyright owners. If any error or omission has occurred, it is completely inadvertent, and we would like to make corrections in future editions provided that written notification is made to the publisher:

BLUE MOUNTAIN ARTS, INC., P.O. Box 4549, Boulder, Colorado 80306.